PRESENTED BY UNIQVISE INSIGHTFUL BOOKS

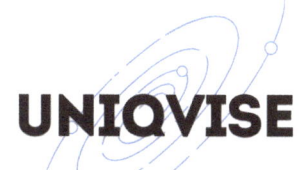

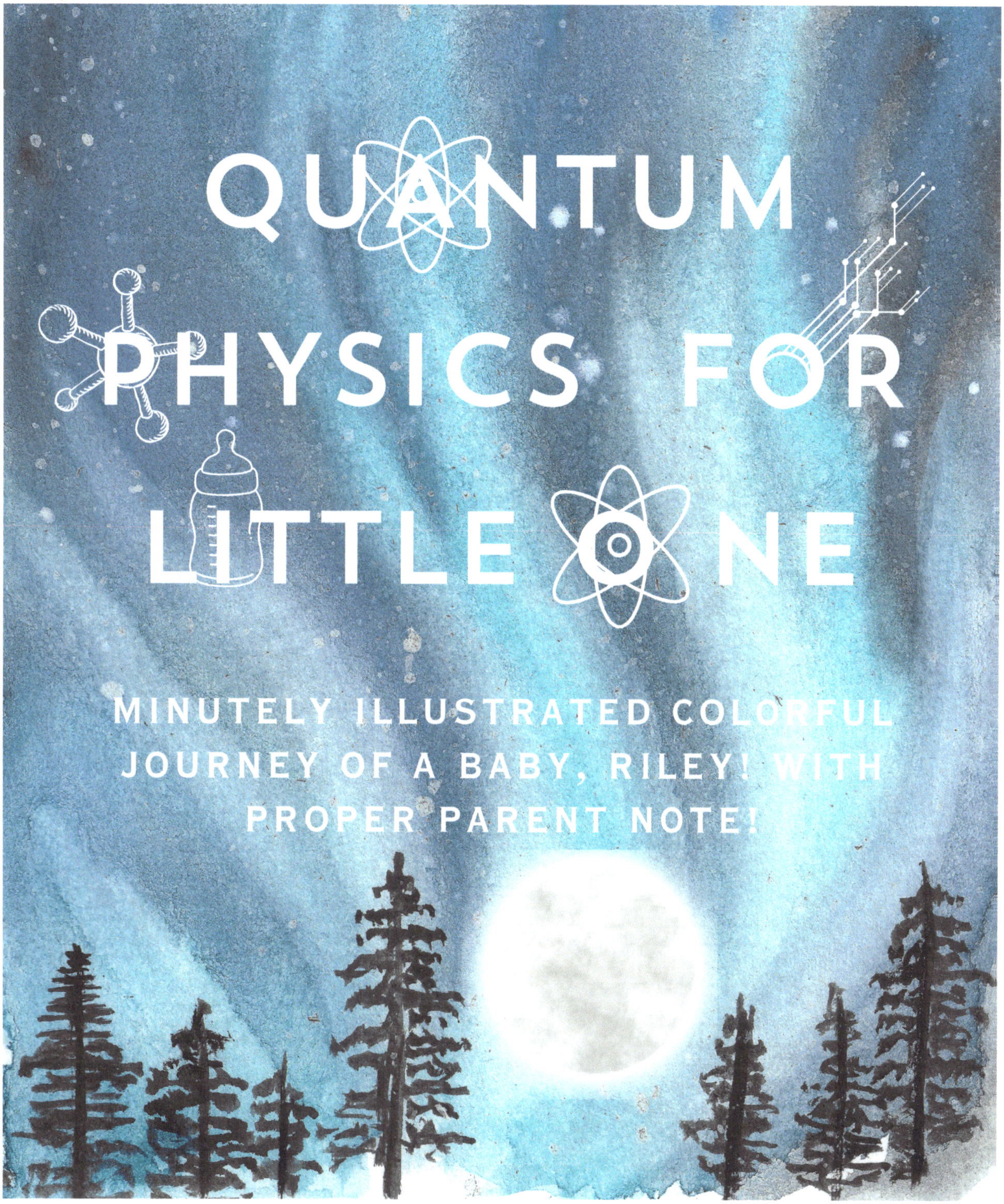
QUANTUM PHYSICS FOR LITTLE ONE
MINUTELY ILLUSTRATED COLORFUL JOURNEY OF A BABY, RILEY! WITH PROPER PARENT NOTE!

IN THE END, AN UNIQUE SURPRISE IS WAITING FOR YOU!

This! My birth mark, isn't it cool!

Hello! Little one, I'm Riley. Let us walk together in the tiny world of Quantum Physics!

PARENT NOTE

Look in the sky or in the garden, whatever you can see are like your friends and wanted to share with you, what's inside of them! All set!

We don't stop here in this tiny but wonder world! These atoms are made up of even tinier pieces called particles. And they are of 3 types mainly:

Protons and neutrons in the center (we call them nucleus); outside which electrons revolve around.

Say hi to each type that I gave below!

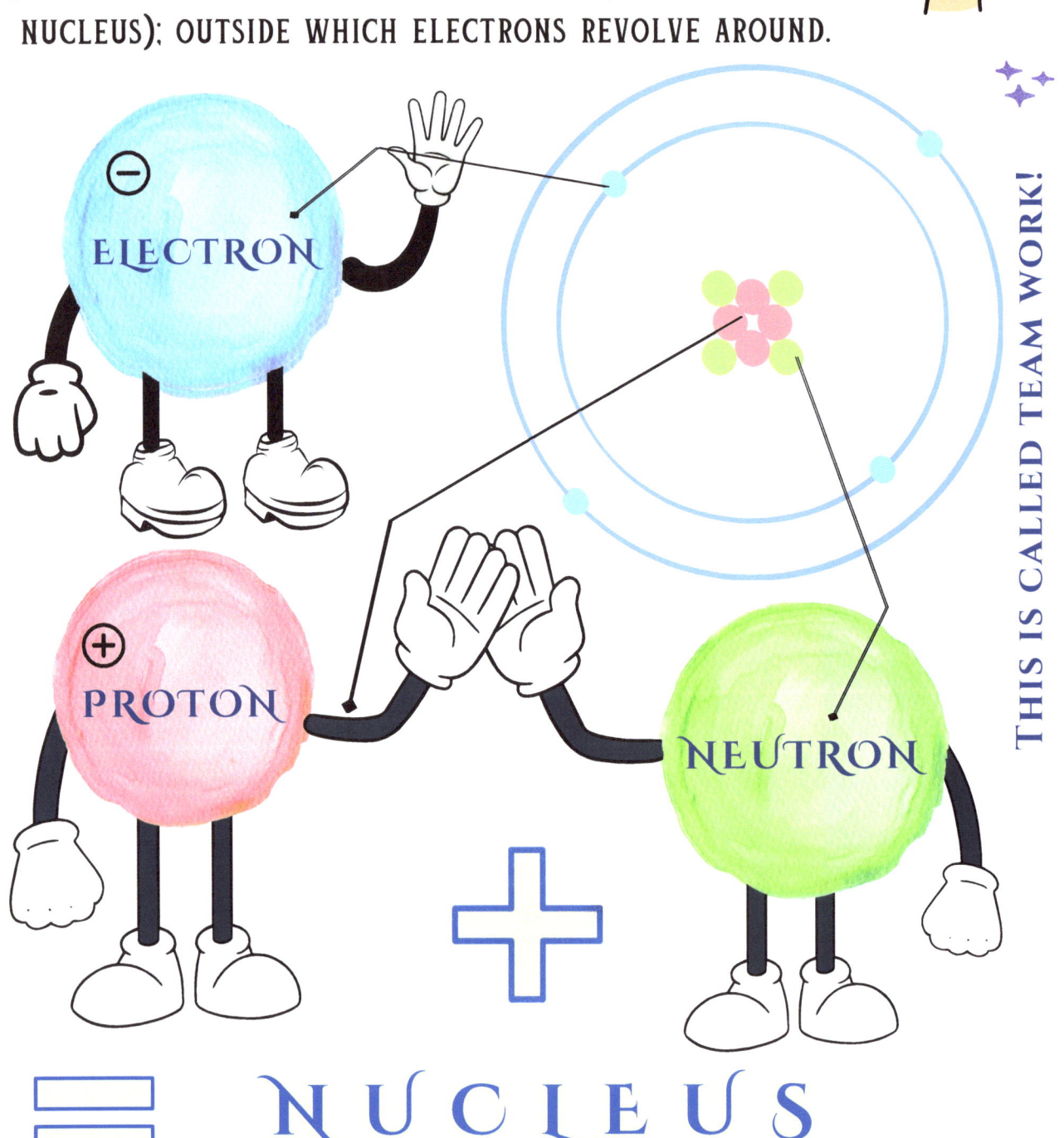

ELECTRON

PROTON + NEUTRON = NUCLEUS

THIS IS CALLED TEAM WORK!

Light, like the sunshine and the light from lamps, can behave like both a wave and a particle.

That means it can travel in waves or as tiny bits of energy called photons!

"Isn't light amazing", said Riley. "It can act like both a wave in the ocean and a tiny particle. Let's slide to see how it changes!"

Wave-Particle Duality: Light can behave like both waves and particles, depending on how we look at it!

PARENT NOTE

In the tiny world of quantum physics, things can be in more than one place at the same time! This is called superposition. Superposition means that tiny particles, like the ones that make up everything around us, can exist in multiple states at once until we look at them.

Throw a dice! It will be showing different numbers.

I show you two side of mine, four and five, it's on you to choose side to see.

Imagine, In the quantum world, things can be in two different places or states at once. It's like I'm Riley but disguised as dinosaur!

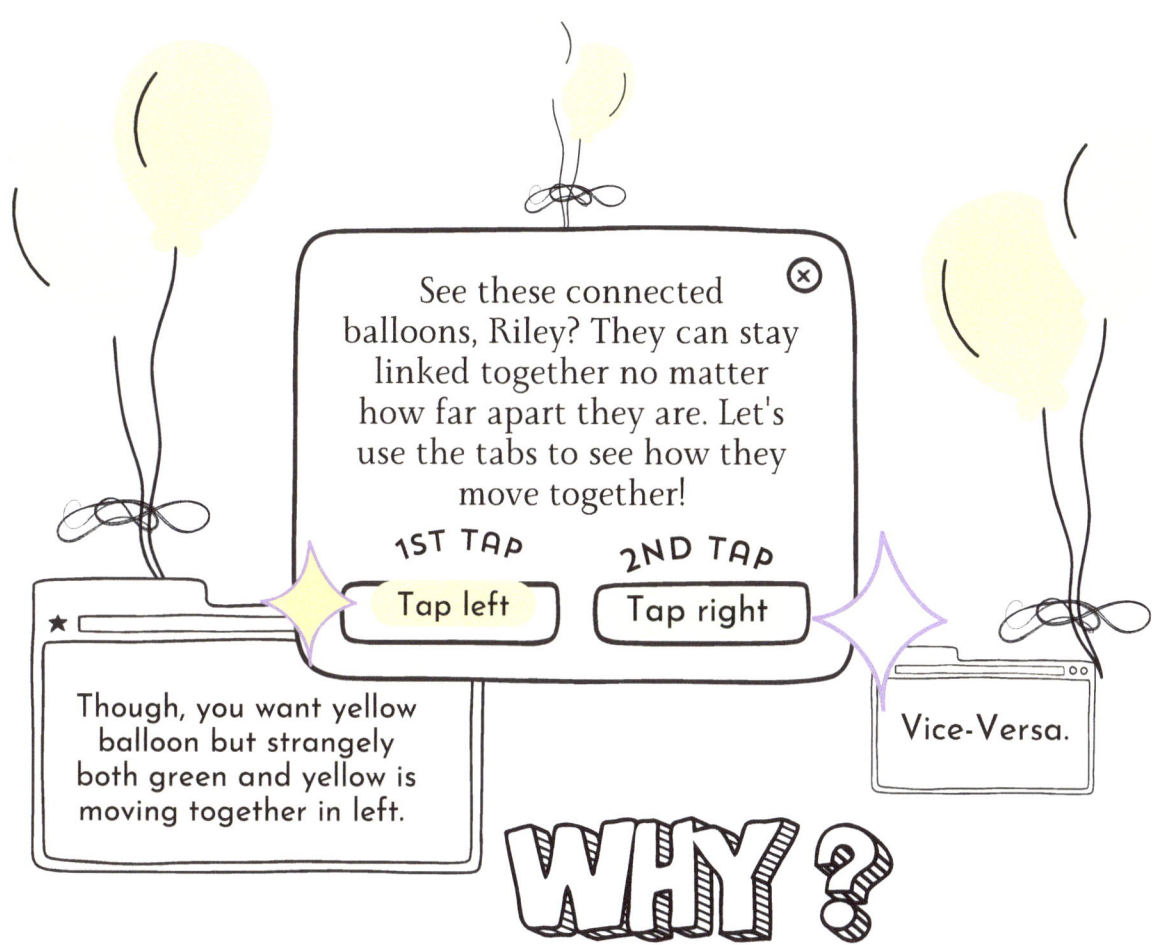

See these connected balloons, Riley? They can stay linked together no matter how far apart they are. Let's use the tabs to see how they move together!

1ST TAP — Tap left
2ND TAP — Tap right

Though, you want yellow balloon but strangely both green and yellow is moving together in left.

Vice-Versa.

WHY?

SOMETIMES, PARTICLES CAN BECOME CONNECTED IN A SPECIAL WAY CALLED QUANTUM ENTANGLEMENT. EVEN IF THEY ARE FAR APART, WHAT HAPPENS TO ONE PARTICLE CAN AFFECT THE OTHER!

PARENT NOTE

Quantum Entanglement: When particles become connected, what happens to one can affect the other, even at a distance. It's like they have a secret way of staying linked!

My balloons!

THIS UNIQUE FEATURE OF PARTICLES IN QUANTUM PHYSICS CAN BE USED VERY WELL IN CREATING QUANTUM COMPUTERS THAT IS NOT ANY ORDINARY COMPUTER RATHER THE ONE WHICH WILL CALCULATE FOR YOU AT THE SPLIT SECONDS.

Riley: Look at this little champ! Quantum computers are super fast and can do amazing calculations.

PARENT NOTE

Quantum Computing: Using quantum physics to create computers that can do incredibly fast calculations.

Quantum mechanics helps us understand how the smallest parts of our world work, said Riley. Let's learn more about it together, after milk.

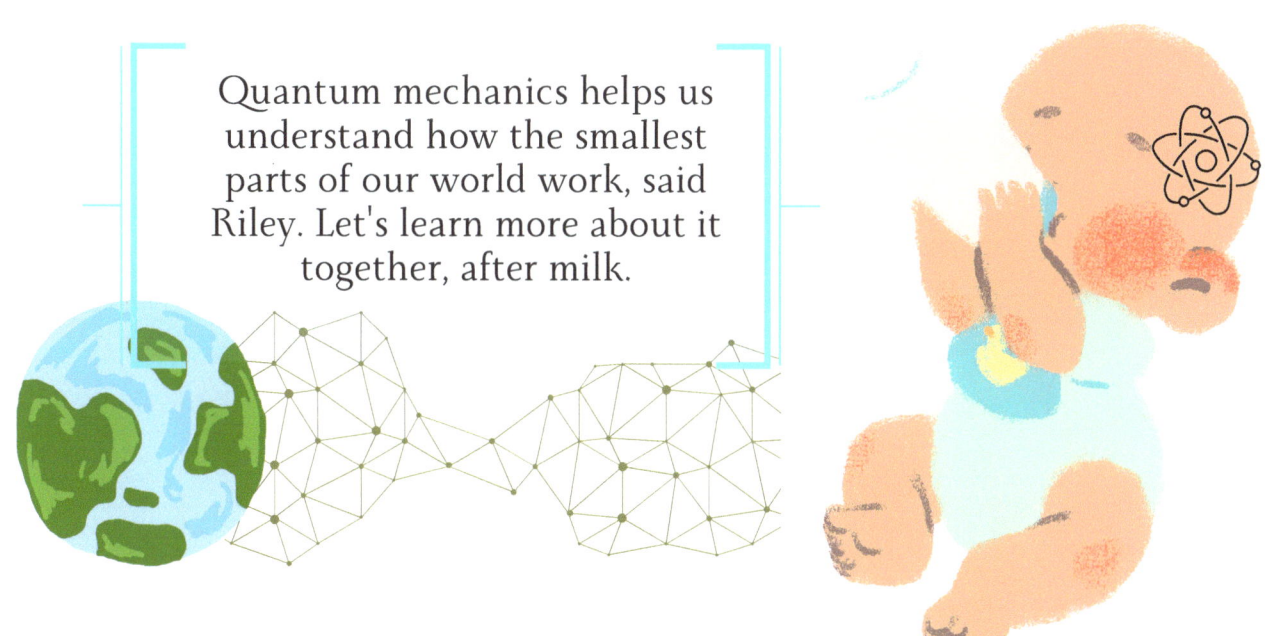

QUANTUM MECHANICS IS THE BRANCH OF PHYSICS THAT STUDIES HOW TINY PARTICLES LIKE ATOMS AND ELECTRONS BEHAVE. IT HELPS SCIENTISTS UNDERSTAND THE RULES OF THE QUANTUM WORLD!

One behavior of atoms is that they can spin in two directions at once until we check on them.

Riley: Look! Electrons in atoms can move between different energy levels.

Electrons move around an atom in different levels of energy. It's like they have different floors they can jump between! These floors decide how the atom acts.

Energy Levels: Different levels where electrons can be found around an atom, jumping between these level to move around.

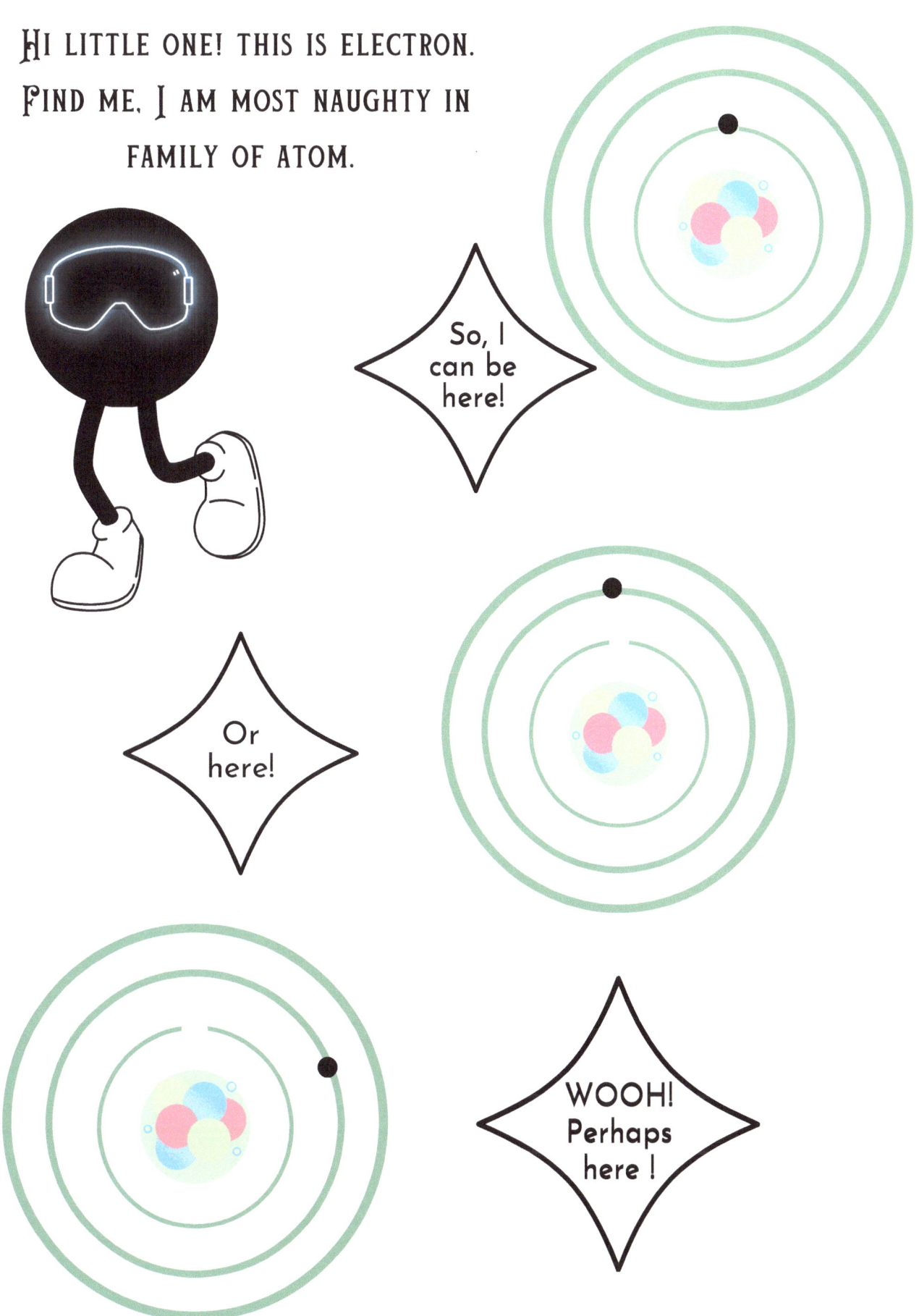

In quantum physics, sometimes particles can pass through barriers that should be impossible to cross. This is called quantum tunneling! It's like a secret pathway only they can use. This helps many important things in the universe happen. This helps stars shine and makes some tiny gadgets work.

Riley: Let's guide the particle through the maze to see how it tunnels!

PARENT NOTE

Quantum Tunneling: When particles can pass through barriers that they shouldn't be able to cross, like walking through a wall!

Particles in the quantum world can exist in various states, like spinning or moving. They can also wiggle or even disappear and reappear unexpectedly. These different states help scientists understand how tiny things work, leading to amazing discoveries about our world.

Have you wondered about flickering butterfly? Random motion!

Can you guess, who am I? Your Riley! How is my suit, quanta scientist created it for Mars life!! How you identified me?

Riley: I caught you, you were able to identify me because of birth mark, right? Anyways, see these states? In the quantum world, particles can be in many different states at once. Let's spin the spinner to see how they change!

PARENT NOTE -

Quantum States: Different ways particles can be in the quantum world, like spinning or moving.

When waves or particles overlap and create patterns, it's called quantum interference. It's like drawing with different colors that mix together!

Riley: See these patterns? In the quantum world, waves and particles can overlap to create cool designs. Let's overlap them to see what happens!

PARENT NOTE -

Quantum Interference: When waves or particles overlap and create patterns in the quantum world.

You can't see ring of saturn from earth. But, we know that after using advance tools!

IN QUANTUM PHYSICS, EVERY PARTICLE IS SURROUNDED BY A QUANTUM FIELD. IT'S LIKE HAVING AN INVISIBLE ENERGY FIELD AROUND YOU!

Riley: Look at these fields! In the quantum world, particles have invisible energy fields around them.

Quantum Field: An invisible energy field that surrounds every particle in the quantum world.

PARENT NOTE -

Warmth of your mum's huggy is an incredible unseen energy but one in universe type! Look at this baby Koala! Aww!

TINY, RANDOM CHANGES IN THE QUANTUM WORLD ARE CALLED QUANTUM FLUCTUATIONS. IT'S LIKE BUBBLES POPPING UP AND DISAPPEARING!

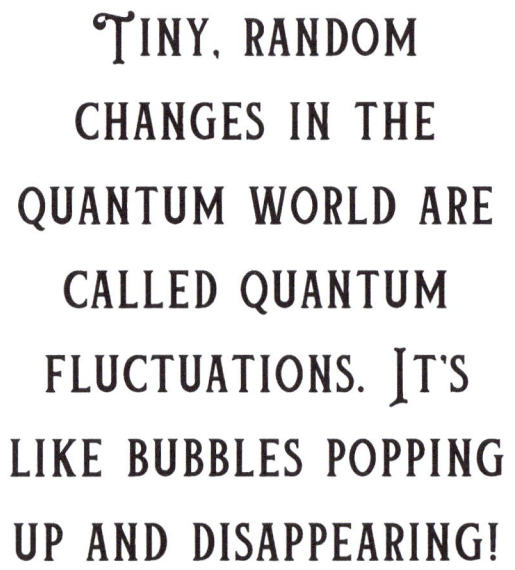

Riley: See these changes? In the quantum world, things can randomly change all the time. Let's pop the bubbles to see how they fluctuate!

Quantum Fluctuations: Tiny, random changes that happen in the quantum world, like bubbles popping up and disappearing.

PARENT NOTE -

Now you're aware about the smallest world ever known to humans. Further in Astrophysics book, you'll get to know biggest world ever known to humans. And we will link both world by travelling with Rocket, that will be your third exploration!

Have you noticed one thing atoms circle around nucleus containing protons and neutrons. Same way but at much larger picture, planets move around our blazing ball, called sun. What a wonder from the Almighty, creator of all!

Thinik about it as sun rotates itself too, do the nucleus also spins on its own?!

UNIQVISE

from the bottom of my heart, Thank you!

CUT OUT THIS CERTIFICATE AND DECOR YOUR CHAMP ROOM!

MINI DIPLOMA IN QUANTUM PHYSICS

This certifies that

----

has ventured into the fascinating world of quantum physics! For your quantum leaps and bounds in early learning!

FOR CURIOUS MINDS THAT REACH FOR THE STARS AND ASK 'WHAT IF?'

DATE OF ISSUANCE:

WRITE ABOVE BABY'S NAME & DAY YOU REACHED HERE!